Dedication

This book is dedicated to my Grandparents Marie Peterson Acker & Kenneth Jonathan Acker.

My Grandma built my spiritual and natural foundation and gave me unconditional love that words cannot explain. She was my world and taken from me way too soon. I can only hope that with this writing she is proud of me.

My Granddad gave me his creativeness and his love of nature. Best story teller I have ever known. Tough as they are but so patient and understanding.

I love and miss you every day!!!!

Thank you

There is two people who I want to thank because without them this would never had happen.

Tweedy Thomas you are my girl!! You are my friend, my inspiration and also my Pastor. I don't know where I would be if it weren't for you. Your laughter is contagious. Your smile is infectious. You live the Word of God in every situation. You are a great role model and I love you more.

Shawayla Johnson you are my cheerleader. I can ask any crazy question and you just answer. I can be off the wall self with you and that my friend is priceless! Love you Elder Diva!

Table of Content

Welcome

Welcome to the "Don't preach but got a word" show! My name is Travis Tongue-Tied and I will be your host! We are blasting away on the AM side of the dial on station Kingdom 1212!

Let me give you a brief rundown of what this show is about! Our guests are you everyday type people that you might see in the grocery store, library, mall and etc. You will never see them in the pulpit! Their calling is not to preach the Word of God over a pulpit but that don't mean God won't use them!

This show will stimulate your mind, make you think, most importantly read the Bible & allow God to enlighten you. This show will also illustrate that God can and will use anyone, and that includes you! Who knows, you might make it on the show yourself!

My job is to introduce the guest and occasionally ask a question. Once I turn the mic over the guest will be in control. Service announcements will be minimal while the guest speaks because we don't want them to lose their train of thought. Remember these people are not professional radio personalities.

So sit back, relax, grab a beverage, your Bible, your notepad and enjoy yourself.

Dirt & Bones

Please welcome to the show our guest today who is Hank the hauler from Hutchins! I am so glad you are here today Hank and I am looking forward to what insight God has given you! Please take your time and don't worry about any formalities because I just want you to be you. The mic is yours

(Hank) Thank Travis. I've never been on the radio before and must admit I am a little nervous. Normally I just talk with my buddies.

(Travis) Even though you have a mic in front of you just ignore it and talk to me like you would your buddies!

(Hank) Okay Travis here goes. I was working in the garden the other day, getting the soil ready for planting and it kind of struck me that God made man out of dirt and women from bone. I actually wondered why men were made from something soft and women from something hard. So it got me to pondering and had to do a little research.

Well, I read in Genesis 2:7 *that the Lord formed man from the dust of the ground*. I know what dust is because I can't seem to keep it out of my house but wanted an official definition. Dust is defined as fine, dry powder consisting of tiny particles of the earth. That kind of sort of blew my mind the He created man basically out of nothing. I really can't wrap my mind around dust but dirt I can understand a little better.

Then I got to wondering if dirt and earth were the same thing. To me earth is soil and that is why I say earth. Well I decided to see what those fancy scientists had to say and was quite surprised. They said that soil was made up of minerals, water, air and other living things. Ok that made sense to me. Then they said that dirt comes from soil but were not the same. I was just a tad perplexed by what they were saying. Well the planet earth is made up of many layers but when you remove some of it then it becomes dirt. In this process dirt loses its identity and dirt is no longer part of the earth.

Let me give you a visual. You have earth where you can plant produce, build homes & skyscrapers. You even walk on the ground which is earth. Now dirt is something you get under your fingernails. You don't have to work with the soil to get dirt under your nails. My grandbaby who don't even crawl yet seems to get her nails dirty. That dirt has no foundation or character. Dirt was removed from the earth and therefore no longer has its history.

So when God decided to use dirt to create man, He basically was taking the key components of earth but removing the history to make a new creation. A good example would be adobe bricks. They are made from dirt, formed by hand and can be used to make homes, fences and pathways, just to name a few examples. Then it dawned on me that soil isn't soft but hard, durable, reliable and versatile.

Now when God created man it wasn't a living being until He breathed into the nostrils. So it's the breath of God that gives us life. Nothing else. It just makes sense that we have involuntary functions such as; the heartbeat, breathing, our circulation and other stuff because it is actually God that gives us life and sustains it.

Then I wondered why we all look so different because it says in Genesis 1:27 that *God created man in his own image.* I reckon He created the spirit man before He created the physical man. Now dirt may be the same but depending on the region it's actually different. So maybe He used different dirt that created the different looks. No proof of that but it makes sense to me. Either way, if He made man in His image it seems stupid to be a racist. I mean if you hate someone just because of their skin aren't you actually hating what God created? Oh well, I think I am getting off track.

(Travis) Well I am going to take this opportunity to have a word from our sponsors. Gather you thought and we will be right back!

(Sponsor) *Do you have a germ phobia? Hate that your Pastor always tell you too high five your neighbor? Well here at the Saints-R-US we have just what you need! We have transparent gloves. Once you put them on nobody will know but you that you have gloves on. They come in all sizes and won't make your hands sweat. So hurry down & feel comfortable slapping your neighbor!*

(Travis) Welcome back! Hank you really dished some dirt. What else do you have?

(Hank) I was wondering why God would choose to make woman out of bone? I first thought about my Grandma and her strength and all the things she endured. Then I could see why God would do that. I just couldn't leave that right there so I had to do some more looking to gain some knowledge!

I learned a lot about bones but will try to make it brief. Bones are alive. They are made of living cells that grow, repair themselves & talk with other parts of the body. They support, protect & even help with movement. Our red & white blood cells are created in bone. I was totally amazed by all the stuff bones do.

With just the few things I have mentioned, don't that sound like a woman? They grow living cells which turns out to be a baby. They take care of themselves & they are great communicators. They are supportive & can be very protective! I was like wow, this explains how women are and I am impressed!!

Now I know man has bone in him and therefore has the same capabilities. Sadly some men don't acknowledge that & place most of the burden on the woman. I have heard some preachers blame women for the fall but when I read the Word both Adam & Eve ate of the fruit. Just a little side note to this. God commanded Adam in Genesis 2:16-17, *And the Lord commanded the man, "You are free to eat from any fruit tree in the garden; but you must not eat from the tree of knowledge of good and evil, for when you eat of it you will surely die."* Eve hadn't even been created yet!

I thought of the saying they use at funerals. You know the, ashes to ashes, dust to dust part, well I couldn't find that in the scriptures but I found where we go back to dust. I found in Ecclesiastes 3:20, *All go to the same place, all come from dust, and all to dust all return.* So our flesh goes back to dust but yet the bones don't disappear unless you're cremated of course. I say that because of those archeologist study the bones they discover and can figure out how old they were, when they died & may even tell how a person died. Well what do you know, it just dawned on me, when soil becomes dirt it loses its history but the bones keep their history. Might explain why women have a long memory and men don't.

Basically, to me, one is not greater than the other because the same spirit of God gives all life but we were designed to work together. We each have our purpose, strengths and weaknesses but we complement each other. If we could just get passed the physical part & focus on the spirit man then we would find harmony with one another. Well Travis I think I have talked enough! Thank you!

(Travis) Wow Hank! That is great and you really cut to the bone with that. So many things to ponder & reflect. I know if we had more time we could have really dissect this even more but this is where the radio family starts their research. I would like to Thank everyone who tuned in today to Kingdom 1212!

(Church Bulletin) Don't forget that this Saturday, the church of the Holy Redeemed Community of Living Water Church will be having a fish fry & bake sale to earn money to help with the funeral services of Bishop Reverend Pastor Cleotis Garfield. They really need to have a great turn out so they can bury him faster!!

See you next time on "Don't preacher but got a word" show!!

Cain Mentality

Today is going to be a great show! We have Cordell, the candle-maker from Crandall with us today! I believe he will be shedding some light on us all! Cordell, welcome to K1212 and the airwaves are all yours!

(Cordell) Thanks Travis dude! I want to talk about the Cain mentality! I mean it's all over the TV, internet and radio. You hear about murders, road rage, rapes and robberies just to name a few things that's going on. Some of them make me very sad and others really make me mad. Dude I got a little self-righteous one day and had this snobby attitude. I was like if these folks had some Jesus in their life they wouldn't be doing these things. So in my pompous thoughts I asked God why? He just said, it's the Cain mentality. This little nugget peak my curiosity and I went immediately to my bible and looked up Genesis 4. I started to read and right there in black and white I began to get some smartness.

You know the Cain mentality affects everyone from those in the church to those in the streets. I am totally sure when you hear the name Cain the first thing that comes to mind is that you know he was the first dude to murder when he killed Abel. Of course you would never think that has anything to do with you because you have never killed anyone. Hopefully. Well it really doesn't have anything to do with murder. The murder was the end result of his mentality. You know that was a deep moment for me!

Let me break it down! Ok, the first thing was that Cain got mad because Abel gave a better offering to God which pleased Him. God is pleased with Abel's offering but not with Cain's. Why wouldn't that please God? I mean they didn't even give the same stuff. Well, in a nutshell, Abel gave God the best while Cain gave God stuff that he wasn't going to use. In other words his offering was just extra he had. Let me use an example in today's world. Do you give the church $10.00 but you know you should be giving $100.00? Now why would Cain get mad when he knows he was just giving God a jester & not a sacrifice of his stuff? Well do you get mad when you see God blessing someone else with what you wanted but you didn't get it? Do you get upset when someone has a greater anointing than you? Just a few points to show the Cain mentality!

Now I am going to show you another phase of the mentality. God asked Cain why he was so mad. Genesis 4:6-7 *Then the LORD said to Cain, "Why are you angry? Why is your face downcast? If you do what is right, will you not be accepted? But if you do not do what is right, sin is crouching at your door; it desires to have you, but you must rule over it."* Right there God gives a warning. God didn't yell at him or tell him he wasn't any good. He just simply stated that if you do well it will be accepted. God wasn't playing favorites He was just pleased with the better offering. Let me give you a modern example! You go to work late, take longer lunch hours & take longer breaks but get mad when your co-worker gets promoted. Another part of the Cain mentality. Are you looking in the mirror yet?

If you aren't seeing yourself yet maybe this might open your eyes. Now then Cain plots his revenge which today would be called premeditated murder. He tricks him to the field & they get into an argument and he kills his brother. Now when our anger flares up that opens the door for the devil to come in. We start to operate in the flesh & no longer the spirit. A good example would be the road rage. Somebody cuts you off and you go to cussing and some take it too far and actually shoot them or try to run them off the road. Not you? Well how about when you are at work and do everything you can to be a good employee. But this other employee doesn't do anything but yet the bosses think they are wonderful. You get mad, walk around with a frown and vow to not do anything and start talking about them like they are dirt. This is another piece of the Cain mentality.

(Travis) Cordell you have put the whammy on me. Need to take a short break for our sponsor.

(Sponsor) *This week's special is for ushers! Tired of folks coming in chewing gum like a cow? Hate that you have to actually hold it? We have the gumtoon in stock now! What is the gumtoon? It's just like a spittoon but for gum. We can even put your church logo on it. Hurry in to Saints-R-US before they are all gone!*

(Travis) Welcome back to the show! Cordell is and will be in everyone's Kool-Aid. So buckle up buttercup!

(Cordell) You know Travis dude, I am all for love and peace but God tore me up about this Cain mentality! Man when everything was done, God asks Cain where his brother was. Cain's response was with typical attitude, "Am I my brother's keeper?" Wow! Cain gives a subpar offering, gets mad, kills his brother and then tops it off with attitude. Cain wasn't even mad at his brother but was mad at God but he knew he couldn't do anything to God. So took it out on Abel. Let that marinate for a minute. How many times have things happened in your life and you got mad at God but took it out on someone else? Just like kids get mad at their parents and if they have siblings those siblings will feel the effects of your wrath. I know I have done it to folks. This mentality is no joke and we all have to deal with it in various degrees.

Here is the kicker to this mentality that was revealed to me. Cain had no fear of God. Actually the only time he really was fearful was when God was going to punish him and even then he really didn't fear God. He feared how the people were going to treat him. His fear was that he was going to be killed. I know that God didn't give us a spirit of fear (2 Tim 1:7) but that is not the same fear I am talking about. I am talking about reverence or respect. Cain had fear of what other people may do to him but didn't have any respect or fear of God. It says in Ecclesiastes 8:13 *that the wicked do not fear God.* I can hear you already saying, "I am saved & filled with the Holy Ghost and I respect God". That all may be true but since we all have the Cain mentality wickedness is in us. Let me explain more before you shut your mind off.

Let's look at Sodom & Gomorrah. This city was nothing but wickedness but Abraham tried really hard to find just a few righteous people just to spare their life. They had no care or concern and sure didn't have any fear of God. Therefore since this place had no fear & therefore no repentance, God destroyed them. Now Abraham feared (respected) the Lord and was willing to sacrifice his only son. God knew Abraham fear (respected) Him and therefore spared Isaac.

Another example was Jonah. God told him to warn the city of Nineveh but he didn't want to do it. So he ran and caused many people unnecessary grief for being disobedient. Now Jonah didn't like the people in that city and that is why he was disobedient. He was willing to die (when he was thrown overboard) than have the people be shown any mercy. Only when Jonah was in a no win situation did he finally do what God told him. Once Nineveh heard they were going to be destroyed the respect they had for God made them change their ways and God spared their lives. Two cities both wicked but getting two different results all because of their respect or lack of fear of God.

I realize you still might not be seeing yourself being a Christian and all with the Cain mentality. Well this is just for you. In Proverbs 6:16-19, *'There are six things the LORD hates, In fact, he hates seven things. The LORD hates proud eyes, a lying tongue, and hands that kill those who aren't guilty. He also hates hearts that make evil plans, feet that are quick to do evil, any witness who pours out lies, and anyone who stirs up family fights."* So if you have been guilty of ANY of these things and know what God says about it and still do it then you have the Cain mentality. You don't fear (respect) God and His word. That is a tough pill to swallow. I am still trying to choke that one down myself. In Proverbs 8:13 it says, *"To have respect for the Lord is to hate evil"*.

The Cain mentality is the lack of respect for God and His word. That is the foundation of this thought pattern. If you add them all up it leads to sin. Thank God for His grace and mercy but we also should not take advantage of that either. There is a saying "to know better is to do better" and with this revelation I want to do better. This mentality has always been around but most people didn't have a name for it. I know I didn't. If you open your mind you will see the Cain mentality everywhere. The only way to defeat it is too acknowledge and be aware of our actions. If we keep our mind on Christ then we won't have to worry about the Cain mentality because our thinking will be like Christ! This will also transform the body of Christ and separate those who speak religion from those who actually live for Christ.

(Travis) Cordell you just dropped the mic. This is why I love doing this show! Thank you my man! Time for me to go lick my wounds. Tune in for another show and Community announcement is next.

(Church Bulletin) The Tool Temple Tabernacle teens will be having a car wash this Saturday. It will be located on Martyr Dr. from 8-3 to raise money for their annual trip to the State Fair! Let's not deprive our youth of funnel cakes and plus you know your car is dirty!

Thorns

Do we have a show today! Glad you tuned your AM dial to K1212! Today's guest is Gilda the gardener from Grapeland! I do believe she has a pertinent word for us all! Welcome Gilda!

(Gilda) Thank you Travis for such a warm welcome. It is truly a pleasure to be here. I hope all is well with you!

(Travis) I am great! If you're ready the mic is ready also!

(Gilda) Marvelous darling. You see Travis I cultivate roses. Actually they are award winning roses. Part of my success is that they love to listen to music. I have tried every genre but they tend to flourish more when listening to gospel music. So one day, as I was tending to them, a song was playing. Please forgive me, but I do not know whom the songstress was nor the name of the song. I actually only heeded one part of the lyrics. She said that Lord if you remove the thorn, then she could live holy. Well I thought that was quite odd but I brushed it out of my mind. At a later date in which I heard another song, that unfortunately I do now know the title either but in this song the songstress stated that if the thorn is removed they wouldn't sin no more.

Well that was astonishing too much for me. So I brewed some tea, gathered my bible and seated myself in the garden. I looked up 2 Corinthians 12:8 where Paul said, *"Three times I pleaded with the Lord to take it away from me."* Which the Lord lovingly answered in verse 9, *"My grace is sufficient for you, for my power is made perfect in weakness."* Therefore the Lord is not going to take any thorns away. Whomever the song writer was did not consider a biblical truth. So technically the song is inspirational verses gospel.

Nevertheless as a result I started contemplating about the thorn. When the thorn was first mentioned in the bible it was due to Adam & Eve. The Lord stated in Genesis 3:17 that He cursed the ground but in verse 18 he said, *"It will produce thorns and thistles for you and you will eat the plants of the field."* So from my understanding, the thorn was part of the curse. But even though the thorn made things quite difficult, you were still capable to function.

Now here is a funny little morsel. In Genesis the thorn was part of the curse. Now it says in John 19:12, *the soldiers twisted together a crown of thorns and put it on his head.* So the soldiers took the curse and placed it on Jesus' head. In Isaiah 53:5 *But he was pierced for our transgressions, he was crushed for our iniquities; the punishment that brought us peace was on him, and by his wounds we are healed.* The physical torture that Jesus endured was for us but with the crown of thorns he also took the curse away.

(Travis) Gilda I never knew what the crown of thorns might have symbolized! We have to take a short break and get paid some change!

(Sponsor) Don't have any rhythm? Don't have a praise dance? Well come on down to 2 Left Feet dance studio! We can help you to get a clue where the beat is and show you some moves. You will no longer feel left out and don't have to worry about knocking any chairs over! Ushers won't have to cover you up either! We have a special right now for 5 lessons for only $99.99! That's right! For just $99.99 you too can get your praise on!

(Travis) I know a few folks that really need to go to 2 left feet dance studio! OK Gilda, now that that is out of the way please continue.

(Gilda) During the break I realize that some would say that we still have thorns and therefore the curse is not gone. So let's look at the rose again. It has thorns but the thorns do not limit the growth of the rose. The thorns do not interfere with the rose budding and blooming. The thorns actually protect the roses from being eaten from animals. Taking this into account Paul said in 2 Corinthians 12:7, "*therefore in order to keep me from being conceited, I was given a thorn in my flesh, a messenger of Satan, to torment me.*" The curse remains on the flesh but not on the spirit. If you notice Paul stated that it was a messenger and the purpose was to keep him humble. You must comprehend that being humble keeps us focused on the Lord and therefore protects us for we cannot do anything without Him.

I recall when I first started cultivating roses, I had a very large surplus of bandages. I was so entranced with the beauty of the rose that I was careless in handling them and regrettably I exuded more blood than I ever meant to do so. For a brief time I found myself more obsessed with the thorn than the rose. Which leads to another scripture concerning the thorn. In Luke 8:14 Jesus says, "*The seed that fell among thorns stands for those who hear, but as they go on their way they are chocked by life worries, riches and pleasures, and they do not mature.*" With time I respected the thorn and was observant and therefore my need for bandages became less. Same with life. If I continued to focus on the thorn it would have removed any love or appreciation for the rose. So when we concentrate on the everyday drama then we no longer value the Word of God. Our faith is weaken and then we find ourselves no longer are in need of bandages but in need of a tourniquet.

I no longer expect the Lord to remove my thorn but I acknowledge it and know with grace and mercy it will not injure me. It highlights my weakness and I know this is where the Lord shall get the glory.

(Travis) Yes God will get the glory and thank you for sharing with us today! Time to get the info on the church bulletin!

(Church Bulletin) This Saturday the deacons of Not a Doubting Thomas Ministries are having a prayer service from 12 to 2 p.m. to kick off the 3 days of fasting. All are welcomed and refreshments will be serviced afterwards!

Here Comes the Judge

Hear ye, hear ye court is now in session. I am Justice Travis Tongue-Tied and Counselor Rowdy, the rancher, from Roscoe will present his case. Buckle up folks because today's show will whip your conscious and corral your ego! Rowdy welcome!

(Rowdy) Thank ya there Travis! Sure do appreciate ya.

(Travis) Howdy Rowdy! Get comfortable partner and do your thing!

(Rowdy) *chuckle* OK partner! You see I was having me some kind of week. No matter where I was or what I was watching all I was hearing was folks spewing judgement towards other folks. Well I am a laid back kind of guy and I admit I let these folks ruffle my feathers. So I decided to go out with my horse Rambler, who I also call Ram, to just ride around and clear my mind. I was trying to process all this mess. I just couldn't figure out how these folks who don't know what, how or why another person thinks but yet seems to be experts concerning them.

Well the Lord started dealing with me about me being judgmental. He brought to my memory the scripture Luke 6:37, *do not judge and you will not be judged. Do not condemn, and you will not be condemned.* Well look here, I know I have judged a few folks but of course I don't want folks to judge me the same way! According to the scripture that is exactly what is going to happen. Well that isn't good.

I have also seen people are quick to label other folks. Don't know nothing about them but they put them in some category and once they do that, they make a judgement call without any facts. Once they do that they feel they are better than the person they labeled. In Matthew 7:3 Jesus said, *"Why do you look at the speck of sawdust in your brother's eye and pay no attention to the plank in your own eye?"* If you got a plank in your eye then your vision is distorted. You can't help someone if you got an issue yourself. If you are quick to point out someone else's flaws but ignore your own you are just bringing condemnation on to yourself. Jesus followed up in Matthew 7:5, *"You hypocrite, first take the plank out of your own eye, and then you will see clearly to remove the speck out of your brother's eye."* Once you recognize your faults and handle them, then you can help another but you will help them with kindness and not meanness. I know when I have gone through something, I have more patience and compassion for someone who is in the middle of whatever.

I don't mean to be a downer but we got to realize that we just can't judge folks for anything. Jesus himself said in John 12:47, *"For I did not come to judge the world but save it."* If Jesus didn't judge when He was in His earthly body, then we have no right to be judgmental. You also can't fall into the trap if you are with a group of your friends and they start judging folks. Don't be part of the crowd. Like if you are with your buddies and notice someone dressed different than you. Your buddies start making comments and labeling that person. Don't join in but actually stop it. If they don't respect you values then you need new buddies. Just remember what Jesus did with the woman being accused of adultery. Everyone wanted to stone her which was according to the law. Jesus didn't grab a rock and started throwing but instead and knelt down and started writing in the dirt. Now I am sure it was like a mob mentality and they were yelling about her sin but yet Jesus didn't join in. Jesus finally spoke up and told them if they were without sin then go ahead and start throwing. He didn't stare them in the eye or yell at them. He just continue to write in the dirt. He allowed them to actually examine themselves. The group didn't throw any stones. The leaders were the first to walk away which allowed the others to walk away. If you are a leader then you have to make the first move.

(Travis) Woo wee!!! That is powerful. Think the listeners need to marinate on that for a minute. We will be right back!!

(Sponsor) Are you a Pastor or a Preacher that wears robes? Sweat like a pig in those robes? Well at Saints-R-US have we got a treat for you! A revolutionary new robe has been designed. It has a built in cooling system that is body heat activated. No more having to have 2 sets of clothes. No more unsightly sweat stains! Hurry and get your very own today! We will custom order to fit you just right! (Disclaimer) takes 24 AA batteries and some have claimed to be shocked once system activates. No proof of this has been documented. We feel it was the Holy Ghost.

(Travis) Welcome back to the show. Rowdy are you ready to continue?

(Rowdy) Yes Sir.

(Travis) We were talking at the break and I think you really need to tell the folks what else you learned.

(Rowdy) We need to be able to know what kind a person we may be dealing with. We can't actually judge the person but we can judge the fruit. Take example of a biker. Rides a Harley, has tattoos, and wear leather. Well this biker could be a member of a gang or just an average guys that like that stuff. You really can't judge the biker on looks. That is where we have to listen to how they talk and their actions. Another example is a tree.

The fruit tree can be beautiful, large and well establish. The tree looks perfect but the fruit it produces is rotten or good. So what do we look for? The sinful nature is described in Galatians 5:19-21, *"the works of the flesh are evident, which are: adultery, fornication, uncleanliness, lewdness, idolatry, sorcery, hatred, contentions, jealousies, outbursts of wrath, selfish ambitions, dissensions, heresies, envy, murder, drunkenness, revelries, and the like."* If you notice the word "works" is plural, which means a person can do one or more of these things. This allows us to see if we are actually operating in the flesh and to recognize if someone else is operating in the flesh. Now of course I have to show the good also which the Spirit is. In Galatians 5:22 *"But the fruit of the spirit is love, joy, peace, patience, kindness, goodness, faithfulness, gentleness and self-control."* If you notice the word "fruit" is singular that means we have to show all of those qualities. These descriptions show the plank in our eye and to see the speck in our brother's eye.

This is going to be crazy and it confused me at first but the more I thought about it the more it made sense. You remember when Jesus was leaving Bethany and He was hungry? Remember He went to check out to see if the tree had any fruit but since it wasn't in season he got mad and curse the tree. Now why would he get mad about a tree not having fruit out of season? We are the fig tree. We must produce fruit even if it isn't in season. When Jesus comes back, God gave Him the authority to judge. So we must produce the fruit of the Spirit at all times. Otherwise we are cursed.

(Travis) Rowdy you just blew my mind! I am flabbergasted! Powerful my friend! Thank you for being here today! Well folks today has been another mind blowing day! I know I can't wait for the next show! Tune in same channel, same time!

(Church Bulletin) The Final Frontiers Parish is inviting all to join them on Sunday afternoon for a wonderful concert titled I need a Miracle with the Tone-Deaf Choir! There will be plenty of loud music and ear plugs will be provided!

Pop Quiz

Good morning class and welcome to room 1212! Today I am the Dean of Kingdom University and my name is Travis Tongue-Tied. We have a great lesson for you today and our guest "professor" is Winston the watchman from Wellington!

(Travis) Greeting's Winston. You have a very unusual name in this day and age. May I ask why your parents' named you Winston?

(Winston) Good morning Travis. My parents chose Winston for me mainly for two reasons. One my Mom admired Winston Churchill and my Dad smoked Winston's. It was a win-win situation for them! (Hearty laugh)

(Travis) I was thinking Churchill but the cigarettes never came to mind (laughs). Ok Winston. The students are ready. So the podium is yours so to speak.

(Winston) You know there are times in life when it seems lots of things hit you at once. It can be work, home, physical or a plethora of things and you just don't know what to do and start asking God what did I do wrong? You are thinking it's karma but what if you are doing all that you can do to live right in God's eyes? I have been at this door many times and I am sure many people have and if not, live a little longer. Well I decided to get a better awareness of test and trials.

I have figured out there are three general types of troubles. If we stop to actually look at the situation, we can evaluate which one it is and how to deal with it. The three types are discipline, test & trials and temptation.

Let's look at discipline. I know that when my folks disciplined me it was because I didn't do what they told me. I was disobedient. This same principle works with God. *Deuteronomy 8:5 says, "Know in your heart that as a man disciplines his son, so the Lord your God discipline's you."* When the Lord whoops your butt, the punishment will fit the crime. Easy example that just about everyone has done. You told a lie about someone. Big or small makes no different. You know you shouldn't do it & the Holy Ghost told you not to do it but you did it anyway. Then you find out someone told a lie about you. Instant discipline. Let that happen enough and you stop lying about folks. This type of trouble is easy to figure out!

Now we deal with temptation. This can be a tough one if you're not careful. This one can trap you really fast or creep up on you so slow that you don't see it until it's too late. The main purpose of temptation is to lead you astray from God. A simple thing with devastating effects. A type of temptation is like what the devil did to Adam & Eve. Take God's instruction and word it in a way to make you question what you heard. We all know how that turned out. Now I will give a real life situation which I would put in the slow category. You are happily married. The perfect union has some changes. You have kids, in-laws move in and the family dynamics now changed. Your spouse trust you completely but you find you talk more to your single friends than to your spouse. You find yourself wanting the freedom you once had but know it is just a dream. All of a sudden you are finding fault in your spouse and want out of the marriage. You keep listening to your friends because you keep talking to them and telling them your business. Of course they will say what you want to hear but not what needs to be said. You find yourself lying, cheating and doing everything you can to destroy the marriage until you succeed. You feel justified by your sin to gain what you think you want. In reality, you destroyed what you had and in the end the voices are no longer there. Your action will have lingering effects not only on you but generations to come. This takes you away from God and even if you repent then you will end up getting disciplined for your actions. Tough road that one is.

The fast kind is like what happened to Jesus in Matthew 4 after He had fasted 40 days and nights. The devil tempted him three times. Jesus was tempted with something he wanted, his authority and something he already had but yet to receive. The devil used the Word to test Him but Jesus stopped all of the temptation with the Word of God. Two of the three temptations tested Jesus concerning who He is. The final temptation was just a desperate move by the devil to make Jesus throw away his purpose for earthly gain. A temptation always turns into a test.

(Travis) I am taking notes Winston but we need a recess so our sponsors can have a say.

(Sponsor) Love your church but your Pastor's monotone voice puts you to sleep? Well come on down to Gizmo's Gadget's on the corner of third & bored because we now have the Voice Changer 2000. This new device change's anyone's voice to something you will enjoy! This will take boring to fascinating in seconds with over a 100 different voices. No more nodding off in church. Hurry down because we are the only store to carry it!! Ear buds included!

(Travis) Good thing we don't need the voice changer 2000 here. I wish it would have been around when I was younger! Ok Winston! So far we have learned that some troubles are because of us and others because of the devil. Can't wait to learn some more. Go for it!

(Winston) Well, the final one is test and trials. This type of trouble is unique. You don't have to do anything wrong to have this happen. This is just because you follow God. I use to think it was punishment but in *1 Thes. 3:3* it says, *"so no one be unsettled by these trials, you know quite well you were destined for them."* So we have to deal with these trials which bummed me out until I read *James 1:12, "Blessed is the man who perseveres under trial because when he has stood the test, he will receive the victor's crown, the life God has promised to those who love him."* In my feeble thinking I was like, great I have to wait until I die to be victorious but Jesus then took me to Job. He went through horrendous events but in the end God gave him double for his trouble.

I know it sounds crazy that to endure some really crazy stuff will give God glory but its God trying to make us better and trust Him even more. *James 1:2-4, "When all kinds of trials and temptations crowd into your lives, don't resent them as intruders, but welcome them as friends! Realize that they come to test your faith and to produce in you the quality of endurance."* When our faith is tested, that is a major exam. Temptations are mostly pop quizzes and if we study the Word of God, He will remind us of scripture to help us. When God gives a major exam though, you can count on Him to be quiet. You have to apply, speak and believe everything you have learned to pass. Just like it was when you were in school. Now I didn't like test and really didn't like pop quizzes but that didn't stop the teacher. God is going to test us like it or not. The scripture that really made me think was in *1 Cor. 4:2, "Now it is required that those who have been given a trust must prove faithful."* God trust me enough to test me. I still don't like test but I know it is to bring the God in me out!

(Travis) Winston I really think you just gave us cliff notes and we really need to do some studying for ourselves. You did a great job and I know that I want to pass the test. Well folks, time to do some digging because we never know when God is going to test us! Have a great day and remember to come back at the same place, same time!

(Church Bulletin) This Friday the Pastor is asking for all the leaders of Second Act Vineyard Ministries to be in attendance. The debate of juice versus wine for communion will finally be settled. The juicers argument is from Hezekiah 4:11 and the wino's argument if from Solomon 8:6. We will have a taste testing afterwards. Juicers have also to be designated drivers.

The Battle Within

Are you ready? Ready for the epic battle that is bigger than brains vs. brawn? Are you willing to witness a conflict that is basically a fixed fight? Well if so, grab a seat and get ready to witness this classic struggle! Our advisor for this event is Baylee the bailiff from Bayview!

(Travis) Welcome Baylee and thanks for giving us a play-by-play of this battle! Are you ready to rumble?

(Baylee) I am ready but this fight is daily!

(Travis) Well we know it's a fixed fight so let the battle within begin!

(Baylee) Have you ever had a question and decided to do some searching via the internet but wanted a biblical answer? Well that happened to me and even though my question hasn't been answered yet, God showed me something totally different. While I was searching, the story of Jacob and Esau kept coming up. Didn't really matter how I worded my question it always led me to them. So I abandoned my quest and decided to read about Jacob and Esau.

So we start with Rebekah being pregnant and it says in *Genesis 25:22 "And the children struggled together within her."* Now struggle means to make strenuous or violent efforts in the face of difficulties or opposition. Basically these babies were fighting each other in the womb. If you have ever been pregnant or around a pregnant woman and when the baby moves it looks uncomfortable and some what painful. Imagine two babies fighting each other. No wonder Rebekah had to go to God and ask him "why is this happening to me?" In *Genesis 25:23 The Lord said to her, "Two nations are in your womb."* Hold up! Two nations? So what two nations are battling within her? Esau and his dependents disappeared but Jesus came from the lineage of Jacob. So I started to ponder what kind of nation are we talking about? Then I realized that Esau and Jacob symbolize the flesh and the spirit.

Think about it. Esau gave away his birthright for some food. His only concern was to satisfy his desires. That is what the flesh does. *Romans 7:5 For while we were in the flesh, the sinful passions, which were aroused by the law, were at work in the members of our body to bear fruit to death.* Flesh is sin. Now you have Jacob that represents the spirit. I say this just because Jesus came from the lineage of Jacob. Jesus still lives therefore the spirit is still going. Now I know some folks are saying that the flesh is still alive but when you accept Jesus as your savior then the flesh dies. *Galatians 5:24 Now those who belong to Christ Jesus have crucified the flesh with its passions and desires.*

The battle within is flesh and spirit. If you really think about it you will noticed that this is a daily battle we all face. *Galatians 5:17 For the flesh sets its desire against the Spirit, and the Spirit against the flesh; for these are in opposition to one another, so that you may not do the things that you please.* I also want you to know that as followers of Jesus this is a fixed fight.

Every now and then I will read something and it just really boggles my mind. I think about it and what it means. For instance I kept thinking about when Jacob and Esau were born because it says in *Genesis 25:26 After this, his brother came out, with his hand grasping Esau's heel.* I know they named Jacob for that reason but what was the significance of him grabbing the heel while being born? I thought about this for weeks. What does it mean? Then it finally hit me. We are born into sin but the spirit of the Lord is on our heels and won't let go.

(Travis) This battle is captivating but hold onto that thought Baylee because it's time for a word from our sponsor.

(Sponsor) Ladies do you usually take two pairs of shoes to church? One to look cute and the other to be comfortable? Well come on down to Bunions and Bra's Boutique for the perfect shoes. Our shoes are stylish and comfortable due in part of modern technology. What is that technology you ask? Our shoes allow you to snap on or snap off any type heel that you want to wear. That's right! Walk in with stiletto's, sit down and pop off the heels to create instant flats. No more carrying two pairs anymore! Great for work also!

(Travis) Well those shoes should be a hit for all the ladies! Baylee are you ready for another round?

(Baylee) Yes I am!

(Travis) I think it's time for the knock-out punch!

(Baylee) As I previously described the battle if you notice that they were babies. Well our greatest battle within is when we are babe's in Christ. The stronger we get in the Word the less fight the flesh has. The flesh ultimately will submit to the spirit. I would call that a TKO. But wait, there is another battle.

You see when Jacob was much older and had a very large family he had another confrontation. Let me read this and explain afterward. *Genesis 32:23-26 after he had sent them across the stream, he sent over all his possessions. So Jacob was left alone, and a man wrestled with him till daybreak. When the man saw that he could not overpower him, he touched the socket of Jacob's hip so that his hip was wrenched as he wrestled with the man. Then the man said, "Let me go, for it is daybreak. "But Jacob replied, "I will not let you go unless you bless me."*

When we get stronger in the Lord at some point we are going to wrestle Him. It will be a personal battle that has nothing to do with family or things. We won't have a list asking for stuff but we just want the Lord to bless us. We might not physically wrestle with God like Jacob did as he said in Genesis 32:30 but we will in our prayer time. We will get to the point that we won't care how we are going to be blessed we just want His blessings. Our form will be reminding Him of His word and stretching our faith until He has no other choice but to bless us. We might come out with a limp but He will change our name. In other words He will change our understanding and people will notice the difference in you. This is why we can't quit when things get hard. We must hold on to His word and don't let go no matter the cost. He will bless us for our faithfulness.

(Travis) Totally amazing Baylee. I have to admit I never put the two together but now that makes so much sense. Thank you for enlightening us and POW we have a knock-out show!! Can't wait for our next show and please make sure you tune in same time, same channel.

(Church Bulletin) Baptist Beyond Border's Ministry is have their annual summer fest. This year we will be doing something different. Instead of the usual baptism we will be having an all-day baptism. The youth has requested to be baptized in a dunk tank. This will help the youth raise money also. Adults are also welcomed to be baptized in the dunk tank as well!

Careful Church

Today's program is going to be, "buckle-up buttercup" type of show! I must admit that this will be timely for all of us one way or another! Please welcome Ziggy the Zookeeper from Zodiac. This won't be a Zen type information kind of day but hopefully it will enlighten you!

(Travis) Hey Ziggy! I have a gut feeling you will be like Zorro today! So slice away!

(Ziggy) Appreciate the compliment, I think (nervous laugh).

(Travis) I know you are very nervous and rather deal with tigers than a mic. I also know you're not sure how to get started so how about you give us a scripture and let it flow from there.

(Ziggy) Well I have two scripture's and the first one is *Ephesians 1:22-23, God has put all things under the authority of Christ and has made him head over all things for the benefit of the church. And the church is his body; it is made full and complete by Christ, who fills all things everywhere with himself.* The second scripture is *Galatians 2:20, My old self has been crucified with Christ. It is no longer I who live, but Christ who lives in me.*

I want to show that each person is the church. The church isn't just a building we go to. As believers where ever we go we represent the church therefore we represent Christ. With this knowledge we must be very careful of our actions at all times. I am going to give a few examples.

Long time ago, I went to a church because I witnessed how the believers were outside the church. I was sitting there listening to the preacher when a family came in and sat down. They looked weary probably from traveling since it was summer. The pastor stopped his message to point this family out because they didn't have on their "church clothes". The pastor humiliated this family so bad until they had no choice but to leave. Once they left the pastor continued on with his message. I thought to myself that there was no God here and never went back. Careful church!

Once I went to a street Halloween party. At this time I really didn't have anything to do with church. All kinds of people were there and having a great time. Walking around I saw a group of people who claimed to be Christians. They were yelling and screaming telling everyone within ear shot they were going to hell. There was so much anger and hate coming from these people. Of course many arguments broke out against the party goers and the imposters of God. I have never seen so much hate coming from people who say they love God. I listened to what they said and realized there was no God with them. Careful church!

Many years later I found myself seeking God again. I decided to go to a friend's church. My first visit the ushers were extremely rude but I didn't pay much attention to them since I wanted to hear the Word. I went back and by the third time I realized that the preacher kept preaching the same thing week after week. I was wondering if that is all he knew. As I was leaving a Deacon came up to me and told me not to come back because they didn't want my kind there. To this day I don't know what "kind" that is but I never went back! Careful church!

Then I met a lady on my job. She always had a smile on her face, a laugh to give and just a warm person. Something was different about her. I didn't know until later she was an evangelist. One day I was in loads of pain and out of nowhere she shows up & asked if she could pray for me. I looked at her like she was crazy but I said ok. She laid her hands on me and prayed and the pain went away. Now I knew I wanted to hear her preach but I knew I didn't want to go to any church. Then she told me she was leaving to start her own church. Well I told her I would go just so I could hear her. I thought it was just going to be a onetime deal but I have been with her ever since. See if you're not careful church you will lose those who really need God but if you are careful then you can bring lost souls back!

(Travis) Ziggy you put the whammy on us! I see that with me being the church I must be careful if all that I do because I don't know who is watching me. I know you're not done so take in a breather while we hear from our sponsors.

(Sponsor) Need to pick up some blessed oil and air freshener? Come on down to Saint-R-Us and pick up your scented blessed oil. Made from the finest oil's and scents available. This isn't sold anywhere but here! We have rose, sandalwood and vanilla scents to name a few. If you are not the type to use oil then we also have colored and scented Holy water! Hurry down and smell how blessed you are! (Oil and water comes already blessed for immediate use)

(Travis) I might pick me up some lavender oil! That would be calming. Ok Ziggy now let's get back on this mic to help the church out some more!

(Ziggy) What got me started on this journey was when a few people on social media stated that they were questioning their faith. I was thinking how do you do that? Then I realized they weren't questioning their faith but their religion. It says in *Romans 3:23 for all have sinned and come short of the glory of the Lord* but yet depending on your race, money or status then they put value on the sin. If you are rich then they can overlook your sin as an example. That creates a conflict to the believer who is truly seeking God.

Careful church! *Matthew 7:15 beware of false prophets, which come to you in sheep's clothing, but inwardly they are ravenous wolves.* There are some people who are preachers who speaking from the Word but yet are leading folks away from Christ. That is why it is so important for you as a believer to study the Word so you don't fall prey to these wolves. *Matthew 24:24 for there shall arise false Christs, and false prophets, and shall shew great signs and wonders; insomuch that, if it were possible, they shall deceive the very elect.* The elect is the believer.

Careful church! Some preachers are pimping the pulpit. Some preachers also try to hustle God and prostitute the pews. *2 Corinthians 11:13-15 for such people are false apostles, deceitful workers, masquerading as apostles of Christ. And no wonder, for Satan himself masquerades as an angel of light. It is not surprising, then, if his servants also masquerade as servants of righteousness. Their end will be what their actions deserve.*

Do you know how to be careful from these wolves? Ask God for wisdom. *James 1:5 If any of you lacks wisdom, you should ask God, who gives generously to all without finding fault, and it will be given to you.* Study the Word of God for yourself and that will keep you grounded and less likely to be led astray. Check the fruit. *Matthew 7:20 thus, by their fruit you will recognize them.* Remember it was a disciple, Judas, and the Pharisees who happen to be Jesus' enemies.

Careful church who is feeding you and allow the love of Jesus to shine for those who are in darkness.

(Travis) Outstanding Ziggy. I know this was difficult but warning does come before the storm and we know we are in the last days and must be very careful. Well this was two-fold type word today. Can't wait for our next show! Tootles!!

(Church Bulletin) Lifeline Tribe Ministries is having their annual senior festival at 1400 History road. We will have food, bingo and events just for the seniors. The popular wheelchair race will be held even though last year it turned into demolition derby. We have implemented some safety precautions. We have a new event called denture toss but don't worry, the contestant's won't be using their own!

Nothing to Lose

Thanks for tuning in and trust me you will be glad you did. Today we have Lance the landscaper from Latch! I truly believe what he has to say will give you a backbone at any given time!

(Travis) Glad you are here Lance and now it's time to sow seeds of courage!

(Lance) You know Travis at times in your life you will run across a scripture that you will rely in many ways. This is my scripture, *2 Kings 7:3-4, now there were four men with leprosy at the entrance of the gate. They said to each other, "Why stay here until we die? If we say, 'we'll go into the city' the famine is there, and we will die. And if we stay here, we will die. So let's go to the Arameans and surrender. If they spare us, we live; if they kill us then we die."* I realized that these guys had nothing to lose. They acknowledge that if they stayed right there, they were going to die. Period. So staying where they were wasn't going to change their situation. They had to make a choice. Notice they weighed the situation before they acted. Let me give you an example. I already had a car but the Lord told me to go to a dealership. I went back and forth on this and came up with all kind of reasons not to go. When I did go, I prepared my car to be traded. You see I used this scripture and decided to go because I had nothing to lose. If I didn't get a car then my current car was cleaned out. Nothing to lose!

Now I also observed that theses dudes were locked out of the city because they had leprosy. There is also a famine which affected everyone including those in the city. Aren't we like that? I mean our famine could be physically, mentally, emotionally or spiritually but we lock people out because we think they are in a worse condition than us. We don't get want to get "infected" by them. On the flip side, we can be shut out because we are different and those who put up walls to keep us out are in the same boat. By either shutting folks out or getting shut out we all lose. So what do we do?

There is two ways you can deal with it. You can stay in that situation, also known as your comfort zone and die, or you can step into the unknown just to see what will happen. Here is an example. You are at a dead end job but you also hate looking for work you don't want to go through the process anymore. You have a talent either landscaping, cooking or whatever. You are tired of working for someone else! Well start a business. Do it nights & weekends or whenever you aren't working just to get yourself established.

Then at some point you can be doing what you love and still make money. You have nothing to lose!

(Travis) I am getting encouraged Lance. I also need to get paid so we need to have a word from our sponsor!

(Sponsor) Are you a traveling preacher who don't always have a musician available? Well come on down to Gizmo's Gadget for our Musician–in-a-box. We can program this box to play dramatic music when you want to get a point across or have shout music playing while you preach because you know you can't preach! We can do it all! Disclaimer-can never replace real musician and won't help you preach better.

(Travis) Gizmo's Gadget's really do have all the gadgets! Come on Lance and do your thing!

(Lance) Sounds like they think outside the box! (laughs) Ok so you might be concerned that you might be on the losing end if you step out of your comfort zone. You think about all your past disappointments and it makes you hesitate. I get it. I am the same way. You might think if you go apply for another job & you won't get it, but just remember you still have your current one. Lost nothing. You tried to be friendly with the grumpy neighbor and they growl back, lost nothing! As I said earlier I went to the car dealership just like I was told. Just smiled and haggled for fun and ended up driving off in a brand new car. I had nothing to lose but I gained.

If you read on in 2 Kings Chapter 7 you will see that when the men went to the enemy's camp God made the army think they were being attacked by another army. They took off and left everything. These men went into the tents and ate and drank and got a whole bunch of goodies also. It also says they hid the stuff they found. Sometimes we get blessed and we don't want anyone to know. Usually because we have been in dire straits for so long and also since we have also been shut out.

Even these men came to their senses and realized that what they were doing was wrong. Remember the stuff they found supplied an army so they knew it could take care of the city. They went back and told them. Tell people how you were blessed. You don't know who that can help. Just stepping out of your comfort zone with the mind set you have nothing to lose and you just might end up saving someone's life. Never know what God will do but you have nothing to lose by doing it.

(Travis) I am so excited and have the courage to step out of my comfort zone just because I have nothing to lose. Thank you Lance and can't wait for the next show!

(Church Bulletin) The Revealed Translators Church book club known as the Manuscript Maniac's will be hosting their monthly meeting. The meeting know as Munch & Mumble will be held at the Mexican Manicotti Restaurant this Saturday at five o'clock sharp.

Blood Tales

Hello my friends! Today will be an unusual day. Hard to describe what will happen but please don't turn that dial. Open your mind and see the unseen! Greeting's to our guest Anabella the animator from Antioch!

(Travis) Anabella I hope you are hunky-dory today. I know that you are very unique in what you are about to talk about but I am thrilled with the variety!

(Anabella) Thank you. I do have an unusual way of thinking about things which makes it quite right for my line of work! As I had hinted, when we spoke before the show, that the Lord will your unusual things to get me to study His word. Therefore when He said vampire it actually made me laugh. Considering He said this during communion and I do hope you listeners stay with us. Now of course the significance of the vampire & communion is blood.

So let's start with the Old Testament. In *Exodus 12:7, then they are to take some of the blood and put it on the sides and tops of the doorframes*. Why you may ask? I continue in *Exodus 12:13, the blood will be a sign for you on the houses where you are, and when I see the blood, I will pass over you. No destructive plaque will touch you*. A critical function of the blood is to protect us. I am sure you have heard a preacher say, "I plead the blood" over my household, finances or anything that needs protection. We are asking God to Passover and do no harm.

You must have knowledge in how the blood works otherwise you are speaking with no authority. I truly didn't understand this concept until the Lord revealed it to me in this manner. I am not saying go kill a lamb and take the actual blood and put it on people or things. You see with Jesus as the sacrifice we don't have to use animals anymore. The principle still applies.

Why the use of blood? In *Leviticus 17:11* it states, "*For the life of the creature is in the blood, and I have given it to you to make atonement for yourselves on the altar; it is the blood that makes atonement for one's life.*" Atonement basically means to ask forgiveness for our sins. Life is in the blood. It also says in *Hebrews 9:22 in fact the law requires that nearly everything be cleansed with blood, and without the shedding of blood there is no forgiveness*. Blood is life and also without it we also have no forgiveness. So God uses blood to offer protection and forgiveness.

(Travis) Anabella I am starting to understand where you are going but we need to pause for a few for a word from our sponsors.

(Sponsor) Pastors have you ever found yourself in a pickle when asked to provide music for a funeral? Find yourself having to officiate for someone you know isn't going to Heaven? We have the solution at Saints-R-Us. We have a new CD called the Sinners Serenade. Music played by anointed organists with tunes such as, "running with the devil" or "highway to hell" just to name a few. Not sure which way the deceased is going then you can even choose hit songs like "another one bites the dust" and many other hits. This is a two CD set for only $29.99!

(Travis) I might buy that just to hear those songs played by an organ. Anabella I guess I could say you're back on the blood trail. (ba-dum-bum)

(Anabella) Yes I am on the trail to tell more of the blood tales.

(Travis) Oh that's good! You win!

(Anabella) (laughs) Back to being serious. Seeing that all this started during communion I must investigate this further. In *John 6:53 Jesus said to them, "Very truly I tell you, unless you eat the flesh of the Son of Man and drink his blood, you have no life in you."* If this doesn't sound like cannibalism mixed with a little vampire then I don't know. In the natural this sounds kind of creepy but this is a spiritual thing. I want to give a quick look at the bread part first. In *Matthew 26:26 Jesus took bread, and when had given thanks, he broke it and gave it to his disciples, saying "Take and eat: this is my body."* What caught my attention was that he broke the bread. So he was illustrating that his body was to going be broken which it was by him being crucified for our sins. What he endured in the physical allows us to give him our brokenness. By us eating his flesh (bread) it give us life and wholeness. We transfer our inequities from us to him. How cool is that!

When you think vampire you think immortality but yet a vampire still can die. A vampire also takes blood usually killing their victim. When we partake in communion we are taking from the Lord but He gives in return. He gives us forgiveness, His power, His healing to name a few. It symbolizes we need more Jesus in our lives. This is why it is so important to understand what communion really is.

Paul gave us a warning in *1 Corinthians 11:27 so then whoever eats the bread and drinks the cup of the Lord in an unworthy manner will be guilty of sinning against the body and blood of the Lord.* I once struggled with this because I felt I was unworthy. What the Lord showed me was once I accepted Christ into my life I became worthy. That doesn't mean I can sin & take communion in good faith. I have to ask God for forgiveness.

I almost went off on another trail but let me get back to the blood tale. Jesus shed his blood seven times. Seven symbolizes completeness and perfection. This means the sacrifice that was made was perfect and sealed our eternal life. Our body may die but our spirit will not. With this perfection it allows us to be perfect. Don't get me wrong we will sin but we are unable to sin with a clear mind. The Lord will convict us. That's why communion is so important. It refreshes us and strengthen us to handle this life.

The blood is protection, forgiveness and resurrection. Jesus did all of that for us. Vampires may be romanticized but the true romance is with Jesus and what He did for us.

(Travis) This is just proof that God will speak to us in ways that we will understand Him and to learn His Word. Great job Anabella. I have a new appreciation for the blood of Christ. Great show but now we must go.

(Church Bulletin) Purpose in Action Ministries will be holding a workshop for preachers on how to lay hands. You will learn proper ways so as not to give sinners or saint's whiplash but still slay them. This weekend only! Hurry down to 1515 Sham Street. Admission is only $50.00

Let's Play Tag

Yowzah do we have a show today! This show will be very different but miraculous just the same. We have three guests today. That's right three. We are playing tag but just a little varied. When one guest is done they will tag the next guess. The show is just a little unusual since basically this is our season finale. We are going to take a break and find more people who have a word for us. So without further delay let me introduce our guests. First we have English, the engineer from Encino. Next we have Shipley the ship fitter from Shiprock and finally Tari the tutor from Tucumcari.

(Travis) Welcome to the show everyone. Shipley and Tari sit back and relax while English starts this show off. English I am excited about today and can't wait to hear what you have to say.

(English) Thanks Travis and I must say I am excited about being on such a unique show. I am going to read from *John 5:2-9, now there is in Jerusalem near the Sheep Gate a pool, which in Aramaic is called Bethesda and which is surrounded by five covered colonnades. Here a great number of disabled people used to lie – the blind, the lame, and the paralyzed. One who was there had been an invalid for thirty-eight years. When Jesus saw him lying there and learned that he had been in this condition for a long time, he asked "Do you want to get well?" "Sir" the invalid replied, "I have no one to help me into the pool when the water is stirred. While I am trying to get in, someone else goes down ahead of me." Then Jesus said to him, "Get up! Pick up your mat and walk." At once the man was cured; he picked up his mat and walked.*

This is one of those miracles that gets talked about in the pulpit quite often. Most look at the man. Some have said he didn't try hard enough, other have said that he wanted someone else to do the work for him. I get why some would say that to get whatever point they were trying to get across in their sermon. I got a different take on it. First let's look at the word invalid. It means a person made weak or disabled by illness or injury. So this man is weak and had been there thirty-eight years. He kept trying for his healing longer than Jesus had been alive in the flesh.

I believe that when Jesus got there the man was almost out of hope. Think about that for a minute. Isn't that just like Jesus to show up right when we think there is no hope left? Doesn't it also look at times that just when we are going to get our breakthrough someone else gets theirs instead and we are just sitting there thinking I thought it was my time.

Remember this man had been there for decades therefore people knew he was there but yet the man had said, "no one to help me". At some time in your life you are struggling and you know other folks know this but yet no one is there to help you. You think someone should at least offer but most likely you don't see they are struggling also and can't help you.

Now here is the cool part. I noticed the scripture described where the pool was. It specifically said five colonnades. So what does the number five represent? Five represents God's grace. What does the Bethesda mean? It means mercy. The man was right there at God's grace and mercy and even though he was weak he never left God's grace and mercy and waited for his healing. That's why Jesus just told him to pick up his mat and go. He just needed to hear the word of God and acted upon it immediately.

So no matter what you are going through you can't leave God's grace and mercy but when the Word is spoken you must act. Don't get discouraged because God's timing is perfect even if it's not on our time frame.

Tag you're it Shipley!

(Travis) Fantastic English! You have given me a fresh perspective on this! Before we hear from Shipley we need a word from our sponsor.

(Sponsor) We have the perfect item for Priests or Pastor's on the go. We just received a shipment of inflatable confessionals and altars. No longer do you have to tell a sinner to go to church when you are at the beach or hiking in the mountains. Just pop it out hit the button and presto they can confess or ask for forgiveness for their sins. Easy to deflate and store! Hurry while supplies last.

(Travis) Well that was interesting. Well Shipley you have been tagged by English so it's now your turn!

(Shipley) Hard to follow but I will try. I am going to take a little poetic license with what I am going to say and hope I get my point across. I am also coming from the book of John. I know we have all heard about Jesus feeding the five thousand but I want to talk about the boy. *John 6:9, "here is a boy with five small barley loaves and two small fish, but how far will they go?"* As English has pointed out about the number five being God's grace so I looked and the number two can be associated with compassion. So it was God's grace and compassion that fed the five thousand. That is just a little side note so now I will talk about the boy.

I noticed there was no mention of parents so I would gather that the boy was probably twelve or thirteen and was at the age to learn about the Jewish laws. I find it funny that this child who came prepared to listen to Jesus for the day but yet five thousand other folks didn't. Now I put myself in this kids place. He is listening to Jesus and the disciples talking about buying food and most likely went up to them. I say that because how would the disciples know he was there with so many people. I can only image what went through this child's mind. I am sure he looked at his lunch and probably thought that it might not feed everyone but it just might be enough for Jesus. The boy had get the attention of one of the disciples to even offer his food. Geez I am not very good at this.

(Travis) It's ok. Take your time. You don't have to be perfect!

(Shipley) Thank Travis. (deep breath) Sometimes we feel small and what we have to offer isn't much. We may not be able to give like other folks even though we want too. We might think that what we have is something God wouldn't use. We must remember that God gave it to us and if we give it back to him He will multiply it and still have leftovers. I am sure the boy thought that what he had would at least feed Jesus then it was good. Jesus turned that small gift and fed five thousand. Don't underestimate what God can do through you.

Tari, tag you're it!

(Travis) Shipley you did great and even though you thought you were not that good you did a awesome job and I am sure you helped many people today! Before Tari we need to have a word from our sponsor!

(Sponsor) Glow in the dark crosses? Yes we got them at Saints-R-Us. We have all sizes. Small enough for your prayer closet or large enough for the vestibule. Richly decorated or simple depending on your taste. If you want to have that beautiful incandesce lighting then this is a must have!

(Travis) Well my friends we are to the final speaker for the season. Tari I know you will do outstanding!

(Tari) Thank you Travis. Mine is going to be a little different. It is more like a testimony for a person who cannot tell it. I am coming from 2 Kings 20:1-6 but only will use certain lines. I know your listener's will read and also know what scriptures I am using. *In those days Hezekiah became ill and was at the point of death.* In 1968 my Mommy was diagnosed with cancer. This was a time when there were no survivors of cancer unlike today. *"This is what the Lord says: Put your house in order, because you are going to die; you will not recover."* I am quite sure this is what the doctors must have told her. You must understand Chemotherapy was available but only for a certain type of cancer and it wasn't what my Mommy had. Her only form of treatment was radiation. Mind you I was only four at the time so what kind of cancer she had I do not know. Cancer was a death sentence.

Hezekiah turned his face to the wall and prayed to the Lord. "Remember, O Lord how I walked before you faithfully and with whole hearted devotion and have done what is good in your eyes." The Lord showed me this is basically what my Mommy did. You see, she lived her life for the Lord. She was a devoted Lutheran but yet we don't have a Lutheran church in my town. This didn't stop her from going to church or being faithful. Her bible was her prized possession. So I know she reminded God.

"I have heard your prayer and seen your tears; I will heal you. I will add fifteen years to your life." The Lord didn't give my Mommy fifteen years but he did give her eleven. Some would say that God didn't heal her but He did but not in the way I wanted. She battled with Cancer all eleven years. Doctors told her every six months that she has six months to live. She was willing to try any new drug that came out in hope of a complete healing. I remember one treatment turned her black and blue from the top of her head to the bottom of her feet. I asked her who she got into a fight with and she looked at me and said, "The medicine but I won".

One time they found a tumor on the base of her neck. They couldn't do any radiation because it was right at the brain stem. Once again the doctor told her six months. This was the only time I saw her get angry with a doctor. She told him to stop telling her six months because she will go when she is ready. Six months later she went to the doctor and the tumor was dead. That's called healing plus the doctor stopped giving her six months.

She passed away in 1979 when I was fifteen. She had a final request before she passed and that was to go home to Webster South Dakota to see her family and friends one last time. We did that and she had a wonderful time. Two years later she passed and all her work came to light. People whom I have never seen kept telling the family all she had done for them. She didn't do it to be seen but did it because it was the right thing to do.

She was a living, breathing miracle. I like to think that all the experimental treatments she tried and endured just might have saved a life somewhere down the line.

Like I said before, God didn't heal her the way I wanted but did it His way. The way He did it made His word come alive to me. Thanks for hearing her testimony with my words.

(Travis) Wow. Perfect way to end this season of "Don't preach but got a word." Don't be surprised if we show up in your town! Thank you all! See you next time!!

(Church Bulletin) Some may know her as the tambourine lady on social media or even seen her on a TV segment called "Tweedy Time." If you think she can play the tambourine or washboard just wait until you hear her preach the Word of God. You are welcome to visit Apostle Jeanette "Tweedy" Thomas at God Is Ministries in Desoto Texas. I promise you will be taught the word of God!

www.ingramcontent.com/pod-product-compliance
Lightning Source LLC
Chambersburg PA
CBHW071759020426
42331CB00008B/2332